Would You Rather Game

500 Questions for Kids, Teens, and their Adults

Heather Collins

D1298699

How to Play:

1. Find people to play with. Friends, family, neighbors, etc.

2. Ask them questions found in this book.

3. The person answering should explain their answer.

4. Don't hog the book. (Pass it back-and-forth.)

5. If playing in a group then everyone answers the question, and then the group votes on the best answer. Give that player a point. Play until you get bored.

Would you rather...

1... be a secret agent, or a mad scientist?

2... ride a warhorse, or drive a tank?

3... own your chain of restaurants, or a sports team?

4... be super strong, or super smart?

5... be best friends with Godzilla or Santa Claus?

Would you rather...

6... have a magic broomstick, or a potion that can change your looks?

7... everyone has to wear sweat pants all the time, or funny hats?

8... drink milk straight from a cow, or eat a live spider?

9... have four arms, or a third eyeball?

10... control your dreams, or control other people's dreams?

Would you rather...

11... have a pet dinosaur, or a pet wooly mammoth?

12... travel to Mars, or the Moon?

13... have the power to control the weather, or a billion dollars?

14... your secret lair be in a volcano, or deep underwater?

15... turn into a ghost when you die, or a zombie?

Would you rather...

16... be able to read an entire book in two minutes, or unlimited ice cream?

17... be immune to poison, or people think all your jokes are hilarious?

18... find true love, or Big Foot?

19... the sidewalks were made of trampolines, or ice?

20... have a credit card with no limit, or be able to eat anything you want without ever gaining weight?

Would you rather...

21... never be scared of anything ever again, or control your own dreams?

22... be able to fall from any height, or run faster than The Flash?

23... be in charge of everything, or never be in charge of anything?

24... see 10 minutes into the future, or 100 years into the future?

25... free movie tickets for life, or free popcorn at any event you go to?

Would you rather...

26... never have to drink again, or never have to eat again?

27... turn into a squid, or a bird?

28... a pillow made of gold but you have to sleep on it, or $200?

29... never get sick again, or the power to heal others?

30... eat a jar of worms, or a jar of ants?

Would you rather...

31... live in a castle, or on a space station?

32... be able to make friends with anyone, or the perfect backyard?

33... a dog with three heads, or a cat with nine tails?

34... find pirate treasure, or a suitcase full of money?

35... never lose at board games, or always pass your tests/exams?

36... never have to barf again, or never have to wash your face again?

37... have a talking cat, or a talking hamster?

38... have a unicorn, or a Pegasus as a pet?

39... an Olympic athlete, or the chess champion of the world?

40... get married in a nice rainy place, or an ugly sunny place?

Would you rather...

41... eat rotten eggs, or rotten milk?

42... save 10 people with 5 years left to live, or 1 person with 50 years left to live?

43... know if aliens existed, or vampires?

44... a dog that can't die, or a house elf, but he's loud and annoying?

45... live downtown, or on a farm?

Would you rather...

46... sucked into a movie, or a video game?

47... never have to sleep again, or never have to breathe again?

48... run your own grocery store, or your own truck stop?

49... be bitten by a vampire, or a werewolf?

50... turn into Santa Claus, or the Easter Bunny?

Would you rather...

51... summon tornadoes, or make a volcano explode by looking at it?

52... have two Halloweens, or two Christmases?

53... learn that Muppets are real, or leprechauns?

54... know the day you're going to die, or the day someone else will die?

55... live in the *Star Trek* universe, or *Star Wars*?

Would you rather...

56... have been born 50 years ago, or 50 years from now?

57... own a flying motorcycle, or a flying horse?

58... binge watch an entire season of cartoons, or nature documentaries?

59... rather be immune to heat or cold?

60... be a great painter, or a great musician?

61... be poor and married to your soul mate, or rich and married to someone you like, but don't love?

62... be able to dance really well, or sing really well?

63... be friends with everyone on Facebook, or no one?

64... be a movie star, or a famous skateboarder with a ton of money?

65... be born into a royal family, or a family of space pirates?

Would you rather...

66... wake up as a giant cockroach, or be stuck in a coma for 30 years?

67... learn we live in an alien zoo, or that humans will go extinct in the next 200 years?

68... fight gladiators in the Coliseum, or bears in the forest?

69... never see fireworks again, or never hear poetry again?

70... be super ugly, or super dumb?

Would you rather...

71... be rich and lonely, or broke and everyone loves you?

72... spend a month in Paris, or Italy?

73... eat pasta for dinner every night, or hamburgers?

74... be adopted by aliens, or adopted by wolves?

75... be able to turn water into energy drinks, or bread into power bars?

Would you rather...

76... own a donut shop, or a candy shop?

77... be allergic to sugar, or fat?

78... sleep in an empty swimming pool, or a bathtub?

79... have a pet kangaroo, or a pet boa constrictor?

80... spend 30 minutes a day on the treadmill, or walking up stairs?

Would you rather...

81... be a famous movie star, or a police officer with a talking dog?

82... a tornado destroyed your house, or it was infested with rats?

83... a flock of geese living in your backyard, or a colony of beavers?

84... everything smelled like cigarettes, or horse poop?

85... malls are only open for 10 minutes a day, but everything is free, or a brand new car?

Would you rather...

86... get stuck in a closet for 12 hours, or an elevator?

87... own two horses, or fifty chickens?

88... speak 50 languages, or be the best cook in Europe?

89... go skydiving or be submerged in a shark cage and surrounded by sharks?

90... be a sports wizard, or a science wizard?

Would you rather...

91... lick the entire bathroom floor, or brush your teeth with toilet water?

92... be super smart, but explode after eating cake, or super fast, but explode after eating meat?

93... not be able to hear music, or not be able to taste anything?

94... have two heads, or have six arms?

95... water tasted like soda or juice?

Would you rather...

96... be able to fly, or breathe under water?

97... have a lion for a pet, or a tiger?

98... be a snowman, or a sculpture?

99... be friends with Medusa, or Zeus?

100... be trapped in an oil painting, or a one-day time loop?

Would you rather...

101... eat nachos every day, or cheese fries?

102... see a car explode, or a helicopter?

103... have a pool, or soccer field in your back yard?

104... there were no more holidays, or no more funerals?

105... never have to set the table again, or never do dishes again?

Would you rather...

106... get in the face with a pie, or a bowl of spaghetti?

107... only be able to eat when the sun is down, or up?

108... everything you eat be covered in gravy, or melted cheese?

109... have a cow that produces chocolate milk, or a chicken that lays copper eggs?

110... everyone was quiet, or funny?

Would you rather...

111... be a full-time clown, or a lawyer?

112... be in charge of building the pyramids, or conquering Europe?

113... be banished to a tropical island, or Canada?

114... everyone always told the truth, or everyone always lied?

115... people have to wear costumes every Friday, or every Monday?

Would you rather...

116... have to eat hot dogs for every meal, or cheese and crackers?

117... be a cartoon villain, or a Bond villain?

118... have a yacht, or a space ship?

119... have a shell like a lobster, or eyes like an eagle?

120... your house was taken over by ghosts or centaurs?

Would you rather...

121... be Spider-Man or Batman?

122... never have to work again, or never have to use the bathroom again?

123... sleep in an outhouse, or in a forest full of wolves?

124... have the power to talk to dogs, or cats?

125... everything tastes like chocolate, or strawberries?

Would you rather...

126... clean bathrooms with your bare hands, or flip burgers with your feet?

127... the internet go down forever, or TV and radio went off the air?

128... only eat vegetables the rest of your life, or only meat?

129... fight a lion, or a hippo?

130... use your last wish to free the genie, or get a million dollars?

Would you rather...

131... always know what time it is, or always know what direction to go?

132... take a trip to China, or Australia?

133... repeat kindergarten, or high school?

134... have lots of money, but unable to spend it on yourself, or have no money, but people think you're rich?

135... cows only produced chocolate milk, or strawberry milk?

Would you rather...

136... fight someone with a chainsaw, or be sucked into a monster movie?

137... trains could fly, or horses?

138... nobody could lie, or nobody could commit crimes?

139... drink 100 gallons of milk, or 100 gallons of pomegranate juice?

140... your food talked to you, or your plants?

Would you rather...

141... pets lived forever, or they had magic powers?

142... be a wizard, or a unicorn?

143... be a pop star, or a movie star?

144... live in a place with sunlight 24/7 but it's cold, or a place with 2 hours of light, but it's the perfect temperature?

145... penguins went extinct, or cardinals?

Would you rather...

146... win the lottery, or meet your soul mate?

147... people stop meming, or people stop fighting?

148... travel back in time to the Jurassic period, or the last ice age?

149... stay home at Christmas, or travel to Hawaii?

150... have to eat your cereal from a coconut, or without a spoon?

Would you rather...

151... be 12-feet-tall, or 2-feet-tall?

152... find the lost city of Atlantis, or proof that aliens exist?

153... wear the same pants for the rest of your life, or the same pair of shoes?

154... share your Halloween candy with your parents, or a vampire?

155... have the perfect smile, or the perfect house?

Would you rather...

156... spend a day at the spa, or at the beach?

157... be a professional volleyball player, or a musician?

158... have fangs, or a tail?

159... be transformed into a talking monkey, or a talking horse?

160... only be able to use salt, or pepper?

Would you rather...

161... sleep in a cage, or in a cupboard under the stairs?

162... learn a new language, or learn how to program?

163... get a new phone every year, or a new summer wardrobe?

164... your closet is a doorway to Narnia, or Mars?

165... know how to repair clothes, or shoes?

Would you rather...

166... your bike can never be stolen, or your phone can never be stolen?

167... be able to mute your ears, or mute other people's voices, but only one person, once a day, for one hour?

168... your toys come alive at night, or be friends with the closet monster?

169... sleep for 30 years, or 300 years?

170... be in perfect shape, or win a Nobel prize?

Would you rather...

171... your hair fall out, or turn purple and grow past your feet every week?

172... never be hurt again emotionally, or physically?

173... be a super hero, or super villain?

174... see a volcano explode, or a star?

175... giant slugs invaded Earth, or the aliens from *Independence Day*?

Would you rather...

176... become a ghost, or restart your life but you can't change anything?

177... travel to Japan, or another planet?

178... listen to music all day, or watch movies?

179... brush your teeth with orange juice, or fake blood?

180... your ears were twice as big, or your feet were twice as big?

Would you rather...

181... build your own house, or your own car?

182... walk through a jungle, or a spooky forest?

183... get stuck for a month at an airport, or an arcade?

184... be someone who builds the plane, or flies the plane?

185... your food was spicy, or all your food was sweet?

Would you rather...

186... be a bus driver, or a limo driver?

187... be okay at everything, or the best at two things?

188... eat tacos for dinner every night, or pizza?

189... vacuum the entire house, or mow the lawn?

190... the streets were paved with cheese, or ice?

Would you rather...

191... be smart but everyone thinks you're crazy, or be dumb, but everyone thinks you're a genius?

192... hibernate during the winter, or the summer months?

193... lose your phone, or your wallet?

194... be in perfect health, or have 100 best friends?

195... a perfect memory, or be able to delete memories you don't like?

Would you rather...

196... get flowers on Valentine's Day, or chocolate?

197... be allergic to nuts, or milk?

198... have a giant okay bed, or super comfy tiny bed?

199... be able to nap whenever you want, or only have to eat breakfast?

200... work a job you love for low pay, or a job you hate for high pay?

Would you rather...

201... have a lame super power, or no super power?

202... change your hair color, or eye color?

203... have a petting zoo in the backyard, or a pool?

204... be friends with a pirate, or a ghost?

205... never have to fart, or never get boogers?

Would you rather...

206... walk on a frozen cloud, or on the surface of the Sun?

207... save the environment, or colonize another planet?

208... one hour of detention, or one hour of math homework?

209... have awesome headphones, or amazing computer speakers?

210... spend the rest of your life playing Monopoly, or Scrabble?

Would you rather...

211... hug or shake hands?

212... run super fast, or jump super high?

213... learn to cook, or learn to act?

214... play football, or watch YouTube videos of people playing football?

215... your favorite restaurant exploded, or your favorite store?

Would you rather...

216... delete fall, or spring?

217... everybody loves you, or nobody knows who are?

218... make money designing products, or designing websites?

219... never eat chicken again, or beef?

220... carry a mini version of yourself around on your shoulders, or have a full-sized clone?

Would you rather...

221... never have to visit the dentist, or never have to visit the doctor?

222... have your beach, or your own movie theater?

223... be a private eye, or the President's bodyguard?

224... stay 12 forever, or stay 50 forever?

225... never have nightmares again, or never catch the common cold again?

Would you rather...

226... live full-time on a boat, or live in the mountains?

227... go scuba diving, or sky diving?

228... have a magic carpet, or an invisible jet?

229... visit Siberia in the winter, or Death Valley in the summer?

230... race across the desert in an old car, or on a camel?

Would you rather...

231... report the weather, or the news?

232... baseball be played with basketballs, or hockey pucks?

233... bicycles were free, or candy was free?

234... see a hurricane, or a tornado?

235... have to ride a cow around all day, or a donkey?

Would you rather...

236... do 20 pushups when you wake up, or before you go to sleep?

237... be in the navy, or the air force?

238... eat fish every day for breakfast, or sugary cereal every day for lunch?

239... have a street named after you, or a school?

240... never have to go to school, or never have to sneeze?

Would you rather...

241... be the chess champion, or the checkers champion?

242... be the knight in shining armor, or the dragon?

243... have fire eaters at your wedding, or belly dancers?

244... own an underwater hotel, or a floating house?

245... books were made of stone, or pasta?

Would you rather...

246... all pasta was chocolate-flavored, or squid-flavored?

247... have mind-reading, or mind-wiping as a super power?

248... have an IQ of 10,000, or an IQ of 60?

249... have perfect vision, or your clothes always feel dryer warm?

250... be part machine, or part animal?

Would you rather...

251... toys were free, or pizza was free?

252... eat grass for dinner, or drink eggs for lunch?

253... sushi was served for every meal, or protein shakes?

254... get lost in the jungle, or in a cave?

255... aliens invaded Earth, or a *Planet of the Apes* scenario?

Would you rather...

256... the museum exhibits come alive at night, or the cemetery?

257... your house was haunted by a poltergeist, or invaded by mutants?

258... go bowling, or drive around?

259... no shoes were allowed in the house, or no pets?

260... everyone thought you were funny, or smart?

Would you rather...

261... have giant hands, or a long neck?

262... have a pet rat, or a pet squirrel?

263... work for a charity, or for the government?

264... be the star of a humiliating video that gets millions of views, or have to wear a shoe on your head every day?

265... walk across America, or swim to Australia?

Would you rather...

266... be a prisoner, or a guard?

267... be able to make it rain, or make the sun come out?

268... the day be 72 hours long, or 12 hours long?

269... live in a full-automated smart home, or an old cabin in the woods?

270... go skiing, or snowboarding?

Would you rather...

271... be born without hands, or feet?

272... be able to talk to plants, or birds?

273... have a hedge maze in your backyard, or an orchard?

274... meet a famous chef, or a famous scientist?

275... there was only one radio station, or only one television station?

Would you rather...

276... your teeth fall out, or your toes fall off?

277... drive an ice cream truck, or a package delivery truck?

278... you can never stop moving, or you can never stop talking?

279... a million dollars today, or two million dollars in a year?

280... be able to change shape, or move stuff with your brain?

Would you rather...

281... be an android, an assembly line worker in a spaceship factory?

282... the internet died, or a zombie apocalypse?

283... have to use a keyboard with your feet, or your face?

284... never get pimples, or never get food poisoning?

285... fight a grizzly bear, or a giant squid?

Would you rather...

286... have 10 eyes, or 12 arms?

287... have great aim with a bow, or a sling shot?

288... only eat vegetables the rest of your life, or fruit?

289... receive flowers at the hospital, or junk food?

290... ride a horse to work every day, or walk?

Would you rather...

291... walk on the moon, or set the record for floating in space?

292... explore the deepest part of the ocean, or newly-discovered cave?

293... be trapped in an elevator with Santa Claus, or your celebrity crush?

294... win an Oscar, or the Nobel Peace Prize?

295... solve world hunger, or find the cure to a horrible disease?

Would you rather...

296... own an entire apartment building, or a mansion?

297... live in a cave, or an igloo?

298... be a fisherman, or a hunter?

299... your parents were space aliens, or robots?

300... be a professional hotdog eater, or a street performer?

Would you rather...

301... wake up at 6AM, or 2PM?

302... have gills, or flippers?

303... it was cloudy all the time, or the sun never went down?

304... work in a library, or an amusement park?

305... design buildings, or theme park rides?

Would you rather...

306... always smell great, or always have great hair?

307... have horns, or hooves?

308... work on a submarine, or fly a fighter jet?

309... be a diplomat, or own a laundry mat?

310... every sport had its own version of the Golden Snitch, or *Harry Potter* was a documentary?

Would you rather...

311... fly to Australia on a dragon, or in a luxury private jet?

312... all food looked the same, or tasted the same?

313... bring back dinosaurs or prevent any other animals from going extinct?

314... always be happy, or be rich?

315... have x-ray vision, or ice breath?

Would you rather...

316... play in the Super Bowl, or compete for Olympic gold?

317... Wake up yesterday, or five years ago?

318... eat ice cream every day, or chocolate?

319... never lose at cards, or dice?

320... always wear a fancy suit, or always wear a bathing suit?

Would you rather...

321... eat candy-flavored French Fries, or French Fry-flavored candy?

322... work in a baseball stadium, or an office building?

323... have a guide dog, or a guide parrot?

324... adventure through the jungle, or an arctic tundra?

325... take a yacht to Europe, or fly a plane?

Would you rather...

326... be a computer programmer, or a hardware engineer?

327... have to wear a hard hat every day, or steel-toed boots?

328... swim in a pool made of Jell-O, or a pool of liquid chocolate?

329... play hide-and-seek in an old factory, or a dark forest?

330... turn into a statue once a day for an hour, or only once for one year?

Would you rather...

331... design the menu, or the look of a restaurant?

332... eat 100 apples, or 100 oranges?

333... own a Pegasus, or a magic school bus?

334... never have to go to school, but you're super dumb, or go to school every day, but you're super smart?

335... win the lottery, or be crowned the King of Mars?

Would you rather...

336... your cellphone was super heavy, or your shoes were?

337... hike across China, or the Amazon rain forest?

338... food or mail was delivered instantly?

339... always have to take the stairs, or get stuck in an elevator once a month for two hours?

340... never sneeze, or never be itchy?

Would you rather...

341... eat pancakes every day for breakfast, or chocolate cake?

342... be the best baker in the world, or the best sauce-maker?

343... everything you touched got bigger, or smaller?

344... all trees were the same species, or all flowers?

345... everything smelled like bananas or blueberries?

Would you rather...

346... have a pet lizard, or a pet bird?

347... have scales on skin, or horns on your head?

348... your hair was blue, or rainbow?

349... when it rained everyone had to sing, or go outside and dance?

350... the world was black-and-white, or we were permanently stuck in the year 1999?

Would you rather...

351... never see the sun again, or the stars?

352... it snowed every day, or it never snowed again?

353... closet monsters were real, or under the bed monsters?

354... be a great surfer, or a great snowboarder?

355... have a telescope in your bedroom, or a microscope?

Would you rather...

356... work at a marketing company, or a research company?

357... be invincible, or the smartest person on the planet?

358... rename all the species of dinosaurs, or spiders?

359... have the ability to walk on walls, or turn invisible?

360... be from the future, or the past?

Would you rather...

361... never eat meat again, or never eat sugar again?

362... dinner every night was hotdogs, or bacon and eggs?

363... maple syrup came from cows, or milk came from trees?

364... have to eat an entire pizza every day, or drink a gallon of orange juice?

365... be a speed reader, or a speed runner?

Would you rather...

366... be immune to mosquito bites, or spider bites?

367... turn into a radioactive giant monster, or a vampire?

368... have to pay for everything with pennies, or boxes of fruit?

369... work in a grocery store, or a corner store?

370... be a police officer, or a fire fighter?

Would you rather...

371... have a jetpack, or rocket boots?

372... have 10 camels, or 2 horses?

373... be able to dunk a basketball, or bake the greatest birthday cake?

374... know who'll win any game, or know what strangers are thinking?

375... libraries rented out dinosaurs, or dragons?

Would you rather...

376... write a movie script, or be an actor in a movie?

377... the things you write come to life, or the things you draw?

378... never have to wear glasses, or never have to wear fancy clothes?

379... mice could talk, or cats?

380... you had to eat dog food for the rest of your life, or drink hotdog water with every meal?

Would you rather...

381... be friends with a giant bee, or a giant mosquito?

382... have to put strawberry jam on everything, or mayonnaise?

383... have to shout the word "baloney" every hour, or "boogers?"

384... your nose was the size of your fist, or your eyes were?

385... remember everything people said, or everything you read?

Would you rather...

386... take great photos, or write great articles?

387... be a helicopter pilot, or turn into a helicopter whenever you wanted?

388... go camping every weekend, or go rock climbing?

389... be a social media star, or a world-famous scientist?

390... have your own late night show, or a famous podcast?

Would you rather...

391... move to a new country, or a new planet?

392... live in the same city forever, or have to change cities every year?

393... live under a bridge, or in a barn?

394... ride a cow into a battle, or a giant chicken?

395... all weapons were made of foam, or everything was settled by rock-paper-scissors?

Would you rather...

396... talk any language, or cook any meal with a recipe?

397... have a magic fridge with anything in it, or a bike that can fly?

398... be best friends with an alien, or a talking bird?

399... never get detention again, or never have to do homework again?

400... phoenixes were real, or friendly neighborhood ogres?

Would you rather...

401... own a truck, or a fast car?

402... carry rocks uphill to school every day, or a bag of geese?

403... get woken up by a rooster every morning, or an old alarm clock?

404... breakfast food is the only food sold in restaurants, or chicken wings?

405... juggle apples every day for 30 minutes, or come up with a great joke every day?

Would you rather...

406... be a paramedic, or a nurse?

407... your car was a Transformer, or just super smart?

408... spend an hour in the gym every day, or spend an hour reading?

409... learn a new programming language, or a new spoken language?

410... have the power to forget any movie you've watched, or a song you've listened to?

Would you rather...

411... start reverse aging after you hit forty, or age normally?

412... live in a house made of glass, or a house made of straw?

413... have a pet bull you have to bring everywhere, or a pet giraffe?

414... never have to do homework again, or never have to eat again?

415... be able to read any language, or speak any language?

Would you rather…

416… live next door to the Easter Bunny, or the Tooth Fairy?

417… have perfectly white and straight teeth, or a great beach body?

418… visit the zoo every day, or the aquarium?

419… take a trip to Alaska, or Africa?

420… wrestle an alligator, or dance with a Tyranosaurus Rex?

Would you rather...

421... put cheese on everything, or hot sauce?

422... there was a statue of you in every city, or a painting of you in every house?

433... work at night, or during the day?

434... count to a billion, or run a marathon every month?

435... always be surrounded by hurricane winds, or poisonous snakes?

Would you rather...

436... all your furniture was made from Lego blocks, or bouncy balls?

437... your phone was indestructible, or your computer?

438... everyone stopped aging, or just you stopped aging?

439... be a hot air balloon pilot, run a bungee cord business?

440... have a summer cottage, or your own car and chauffer?

Would you rather...

441... people had to dance to work, or sing on the way to work?

442... answer 5,000 "would you rather" questions, or climb 99 flights of stairs?

443... sleep next to a lake, or on a boat on the lake?

444... eat different food every day, or the same food every day?

445... deliver pizzas, or packages?

Would you rather...

446... float like bubbles, or run like a cheetah?

447... visit every country in Europe, or discover and name a new species?

448... jump rope every morning, or walk the dog around the block?

449... mice were the size of elephants, or elephants were the size of mice?

450... undo all your past mistakes, or see 30 seconds into the future?

Would you rather...

451... change color like a chameleon, or have armor like an armadillo?

452... have an Iron Man suit, or a Batman suit?

453... lick a frozen pole, or a burning hot sidewalk?

454... eat eggs cooked on the dashboard of a car, or drink lemonade from an old boot?

455... a dance party, or a craft party?

Would you rather...

456... learn the piano, or the flute?

457... milk still came in jars, or people used horses instead of cars?

458... go on a treasure hunt, or play hide-and-seek all day?

459... vacation on a tropical island, or visit a new city?

460... there were strong earthquakes every day, or rainstorms?

Would you rather...

461... get paid to do homework, or get paid to do chores?

462... go to the circus, or the movie theater?

463... be a character in a serious book, or in an action movie?

464... have a pet polar bear, or a pet walrus?

465... swim with jellyfish, or sea turtles?

Would you rather...

466... absorb information by touch, or nutrition by smell?

467... be a full-time babysitter, or a full-time cat wrestler?

468... the museum attractions come alive at night, or the art in the gallery?

469... Fried food was banned, or soda?

470... have an ice-cream flavor named after you, or a comic book hero?

Would you rather...

471... have access to every video game in the world, or every animal?

472... be immune to disease, or hot and cold temperatures?

473... live in the best apartment but have to walk up 15 flights of stairs to get there, or a cozy cottage?

474... eat bread with every meal, or feed bread to ducks every meal?

475... smell nothing, or hear nothing?

Would you rather...

476... milk tasted like broccoli, or broccoli tasted like mud?

477... ice cream grew on trees, or oranges fell from the sky?

478... the hair on everyone's head was spaghetti, or party streamers?

479... giant squirrels ruled the earth, or giant squids?

480... meet a mermaid when you snorkel, or a talking dolphin?

Would you rather...

481... catch a giant fish, or find a humongous pearl?

482... be a private eye, or a starship captain?

483... everyone was a cyborg, or everyone was a centaur?

484... everything you own is bullet proof, or your food never expires?

485... eat snails for lunch, or worms?

Would you rather...

486... be stuck by yourself on a cruise ship, or a space ship?

487... walk on the Moon, or walk in the bottom of the ocean?

488... every party was a foam party, or a birthday party?

489... rinse your mouth out with soap, or hotdog water?

490... star in your own cooking show, or your own travel show?

Would you rather...

491... ride a warhorse, or drive a tank?

492... be able to fly, or live forever?

493... be a pirate captain, or a pirate hunter?

494... be a wizard, or a warlock?

495... dress up in costumes every day, or your wardrobe is chosen randomly for you every morning?

Would you rather...

496... have to sing a song whenever anyone asked, or breakdance?

497... have a magic carpet, or a genie lamp, but you only have one wish, and you can't ask for a magic carpet?

498... another ice age, or a giant asteroid wipes out half the planet?

499... sleep on peacock feathers, or a bed of flowers?

500... backstage passes at a concert, or a collection of amazing board games?

61213468R00061

Made in the USA
Middletown, DE
18 August 2019